ORINDA

P9-CKR-926

WITHDRAWN

Test Poem

This is a test poem.
This is **only** a test poem.
Had this been an actual poem
It might have had rhyme
Or rhythm
Or a little alliteration
Or a b
o
l
t
of
l
i
g
h
t
n
i
n
g

Against a cobalt sky
Or laundry f
l
a
p
p
i
n
g
in an autumn breeze.
This CONCLUDES
This test poem.
Beeeeeeeeeeeeeeeeeeeeeeeeeeeeeeep.

Laugh-eteria

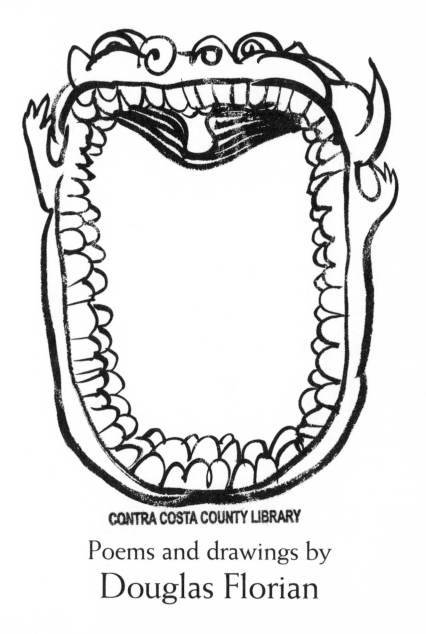

CONTRA COSTA COUNTY LIBRARY

Poems and drawings by

Douglas Florian

Harcourt Brace & Company

San Diego   New York   London

3 1901 03636 3408

Copyright © 1999 by Douglas Florian

All rights reserved. No part of this publication may be reproduced
or transmitted in any form or by any means, electronic or mechanical,
including photocopy, recording, or any information storage and
retrieval system, without permission in writing from the publisher.

Requests for permission to make copies of any part of the work should
be mailed to: Permissions Department, Harcourt Brace & Company,
6277 Sea Harbor Drive, Orlando, Florida 32887-6777.

Library of Congress Cataloguing-in-Publication Data
Florian, Douglas.
Laugh-eteria: poems and drawings by Douglas Florian.
p.   cm.
Summary: A collection of more than one hundred and fifty humorous
poems on such topics as ogres, pizza, fear, school, dragons, trees, and hair.
1. Children's poetry, American.   2. Humorous poetry, American.
[1. Humorous poetry. 2. American poetry.] I. Title.
PS3556.L589L38   1999
811'.54—dc21   98-20047
ISBN 0-15-202084-5

E G I K M N L J H F

The illustrations in this book were done in brush and ink on Strathmore paper.
The display type was set in Belwe Medium.
The text type was set in Weiss.
Manufactured by South China Printing Company, Ltd., China
Production supervision by Stanley Redfern and Pascha Gerlinger

For my wife, Mira Henriette,
second daughter of Raphael Lallouz, O.B.M.

Geet Up!

Geet up!
Geet up!
Geet up out of bed!
Put foot to the floor
And water on head.
Geet up!
Geet up!
The day's growing thinner.
Geet up out of bed
Before they serve dinner!

Ogres Are Ugly

Ogres are ugly.
Ogres are mean.
Ogres have skin
That's a hideous green.
Ogres are gruesome.
Ogres are greedy.
They give to the rich
And take from the needy.
Ogres are selfish.
Ogres are scary.
Ogres say "Pardon me, sir"
Very rarely.
Ogres are callous.
Ogres are cruel.
Ogres don't clean up
Their rooms, as a rule.
Ogres are eerie.
Ogres are hairy.
Ogres are not very sanitary.
Ogres have pimples.
Ogres have rabies.
Ogres have faces
That scare little babies.

Visionary

A monster came to town today.
Its head had eyes aplenty.
This ghoul's eyesight
Was dynamite:
20 / 20 / 20 / 20.

General Gerald

When General Gerald gets dressed,
A hundred medals are pinned to his chest.

One is for valor.
One is for zeal.
One is for swallowing all his oatmeal.

One's from Sumatra.
One's from Tangiers.
One is for cleaning behind his ears.

One is for trust.
One is for honor.
One is for looking just like an iguana.

One is for spirit.
One is for poise.
One is for sharing his games and his toys.

Sticks and Stones

Said Major Moss, upon his horse,
Addressing his glorious army:
"Sticks and stones will break my bones,
But words will never harm me."
Said Sergeant Foss to Major Moss:
"You're fat as a pig in a sty."
Then Major Moss came down from his horse,
And he began to cry.

The Last Piece of Cake

Whoever ate the last piece of cake,
I hope that you get a bellyache,
Or bit when you sit on a poisonous snake.
Perhaps all the bones in your body will break
When you're crushed to mush in a giant earthquake.
What's that you say?
It was me?
ME who ate the last piece of cake?
My mistake.

Licorice Wish

If I was granted just one wish,
I'd wish for a ton of licorice,
Then how my hungry lips would smack;
I'd chew it till my tongue turned black—
All morning, noon, and night I'd snack.
Eventually my teeth would crack
And fall out on the kitchen floor,
Then with my gums I'd chew some more,
Until at last I'd get so sick
That I'd look like a licorice stick.

Giants

Giants sometimes get lost in a cloud.

Giants never get lost in a crowd.

Giants when thirsty can swallow a lake.

Giants can step on a moose by mistake.

Giants are robust. Giants are tall.

Giants can never buy "one size fits all."

Interruption

Last night while reading in my bed,
The roof fell down onto my head,
Which put me in a terrible rage—
I lost my place upon the page.

Grown-up

There was a man who grew and grew.
He grew ten feet and wasn't through.
He grew from Maine to Alabama.
He wore a thousand-mile pajama.
And when he slept in Saskatoon,
He put his feet up on the moon.

Downsize

There was a girl who shrank and shrunk, not only legs
but head and trunk. She shrank as small as any cup.
The sidewalk curb to her was UP. She wore the
clothing of her dolls. The faucet seemed
Niagara Falls. For company she had to
hug the nearest beetle, fly, or bug.
She always shrank. She never
grew—one day she
vanished
out of
view

Unique Horn

A unicorn is born, it's said,
With one long horn upon its head.
I have one horn, but by bad luck,
On someplace else my horn is stuck.

Good Humor

The poems in this book
Are meant to be humorous.
If they are not,
Please laugh just to humor us.

Far Gone Fishing

How do you catch the fish you eat?
　　I snatch them up between my feet.
How do you eat the fish you catch?
　　I open wide and down the hatch.

Watermelon

Yippy!
Yipes!
Green and white stripes.
How I love to sink
My teeth into pink.
I don't even mind
To chew on the rind.
I love it to bits!
(Except for the pits.)

There Was a Young Woman Named Clare

There was a young woman named Clare,
Who kept a large clam in her hair.
    She used it to hold
    All her diamonds and gold.
How it helped her look *soooo* debonair.

There Was an Old Person Named Bruce

There was an old person named Bruce,
Whose dog had hair shaggy and loose.
   Three hours he'd spend
   Talking to the wrong end,
Then always scream out, "What's the use?"

Baby Face

Baby has his mother's eyes,
His father's nose,
His uncle's thighs,
His auntie's ears,
His cousin's chin.
I hope he gives
Them back again.

News Flash

Extra! Extra!
Read all about it!
I didn't take a bath today,
And yet my mom allowed it!

Bad Poem

This poem is so bad
It belongs in the zoo.
It should jump in a lake
Or come down with the flu.
It should get itself lost
Or crawl into a cage.
This poem is so bad
It should

             fall

                  off

                        the

                             page.

Car Rot

Here lies my car
Now deceased.
May its poor soul
Rust in peace.

The Ooze

Down the street
It's coming—
The Ooze!
It's swallowing feet
Still in their shoes!
It's swallowing Harold!
It's swallowing Suzie!
It's swallowing YOU!
(It's not very choosy.)

Gum Drop

Although I think it's mean and cruel,
They don't let us chew gum in school.
But Benton Barton, little pesk,
Sneaked beneath his little desk
And there commenced his jaws to chew. . . .
A giant bubble Benton blew.
It raised his desk right off the floor
A good ten meters, maybe more,
But when the bubble came to pop,
The desk on Benton's nose did drop.
On Benton's nose the desk got stuck—
Though Teacher tried to pull and pluck.
The gum had hardened strong as glue,
And there was nothing we could do.
So if you see him walking by,
With desk and head both held up high,
Remember this important rule:
Don't chew gum while you're in school!

Report Card

My school grades sent my father reeling.
He blew his top. He hit the ceiling.
We patched him up and now he's healing.

Ogre Argument

We're meaner.

        We're greener.

Our skins have scales.

        We swallow nails.

We've lots of warts.

        We're very bad sports.

We drip with drool.

        We lose our cool.

We're more horrific.

        We're unscientific.

We're mostly malevolent.

        We're largely irrelevant.

We're bellicose.

        We're gross up close.

Our heads are revolting.

        Our backsides are molting.

We cling, we clutch.

        Let's keep in touch.

Doing Time

Thirty days hath September,
April, June, and Miss Ember.
Miss Ember?
Why did she get thirty days?
She left the lid off the mayonnaise.

Why My Homework Is Missing

Deep inside my wooden desk
Lurks a monster most grotesque.
It ate my pencil and my pen,
My composition book, and THEN
It started rattling
        clattering
            hissing.
And THAT is why
My homework is missing.

Maskquito

One way to fool
The cruel mosquito
Is to travel
Incognito —
As tree
Or rock
Or anything
That a mosquito
Would not sting.

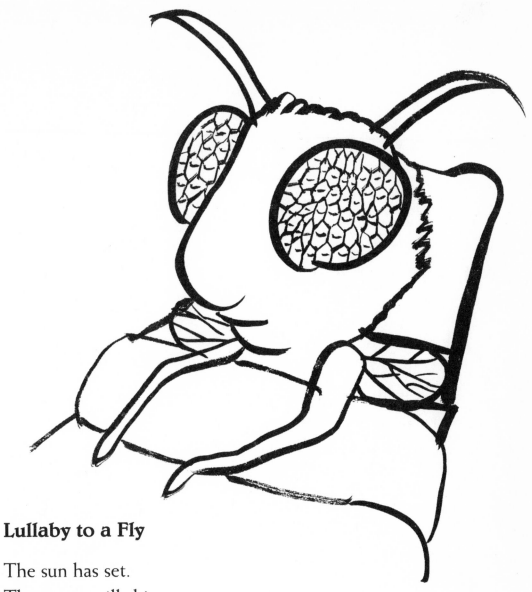

Lullaby to a Fly

The sun has set.
The moon will shine.
So close your eyes . . .
All ninety-nine.

The King Is Cruel

The King is cruel.
The King is callous.
The King is full of hate and malice.
He leaves his toys all over the palace.
    The King is very mean!
The King is cold and ill-disposed.
He likes to step on people's toes
Or put two pencils up his nose.
    The King drinks kerosene!
The King is harsh and most malicious.
He kicks the cat and throws knishes
And never offers to wash the dishes.
    He always makes a scene!
The King will drive his mother mad.
He sticks his tongue out at his dad.
But if you think the King is bad—
    Wait till you meet the Queen!

Pity Ditty

Such a pity
       pity
         pity
Such a shame
       shame
         shame
That I met the
Queen of England
But I can't recall her name.

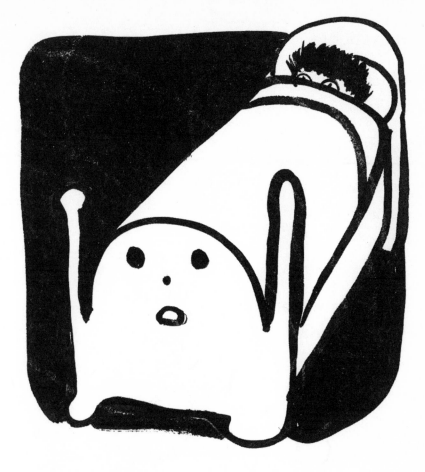

Nothing to Fear

There's nothing in the closet.
There's nothing in the chest.
There's nothing coming up the stairs—
No uninvited guest.
There's nothing near the curtain.
There's nothing 'neath the bed.
But though there's nothing in my room,
It's NOTHING that I dread.

Arithmetickle

I'd rather go fishin'
Than do long division,
Or be stuck in traction
Than deal with subtraction.
I need a vacation
From multiplication.
In my poor condition
I can't do addition.

Let's leave mathematics
Forgotten in attics!

Fishy

Down by the ocean,
Down by the bay,
The fish are really biting today.
They bit my bait.
They bit my pole.
They bit my cousins Jay and Joel.

Graffiti, Graffiti

Graffiti, graffiti,
On sidewalk and streeti,
On glass and concreeti,
And on subway seati.
Some think that it's neati.
Some find it too seedi.
It's really a pity
When all of the city
Is full of graffiti —
Let's move to Tahiti.

Zero Hero

Dotty got a zero.
A zero Dotty got.
The teacher wished a lower grade,
But worse than that there's not.

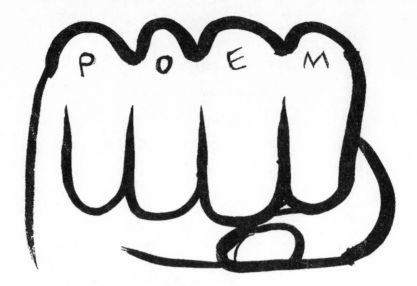

READ THIS POEM!

If you don't read this poem real soon,
I'll make you eat a rotten prune.
And if you stop just halfway through,
I'll pinch you till your face turns blue.
Don't even think to finish here
Or else I'll have to pull your ear.
But if you read it to the end,
I promise that I'll be your friend.

On Saturday, November Third

On Saturday, November third,
Outside my window perched a bird.
He sat there frozen for a week.
He did not move, nor did he speak.
I stared at him. He stared right back—
With wide hypnotic eyes pitch-black.
I yelled at him to fly, to flee.
But he just smiled and winked at me.
He failed to even shake a feather
Through all varieties of weather.
And then at last he flew away—
I never will forget that day.
It was a Thursday, the eighth of May.
I screamed out loud, "Hoorah, hooray!"

He came back Friday, August third.
It's sad how much I hate that bird.

Brush Rush

Brush your teeth.
Brush your hair.
Brush your brother's underwear.
Your teeth are green.
Your hair is blue.
Your brother's underwear—P.U.!

They Gave Me

They gave me a lemon.
I took a lime.
They gave me a nickel.
I took a dime.
They gave me crumbs,
But I took cake.
Life is full
Of give and take.

Batty

The pitcher pitched a pitcher.
The batter batted a bat.
The shortstop stopped up short to see
The catcher catch a cat.

Baseball Bats

Baseball bats have beady eyes.
They're very good at catching flies.
Baseball bats are scared of light.
They don't play day games,
Only night.

Growing Pains

Karen Krane's got growing pains:
She's growing sixteen extra brains.
Her head's the size of Cincinnati.
She's flipped her lid.
She's bonkers.
She's batty.

Poem for Rent

This poem is for rent for fifty bucks cheap.
So, kids, take a chance; the price isn't steep.
It's yours for a week or even a year.
It won't fall apart and it won't disappear.
This poem is for rent, to all who will pay.
This poem is so bad, I can't give it away.

A Mermaid

A mermaid is half fish, half maid.
But something's wrong here, I'm afraid.

Gator Dater

Kate had a date
    With an alligator.
When she was late
    The gator ate 'er.

Wild Walk

I took my little brother for
A walk into the wild.
We met an alligator there—
Now I'm an only child.

Dine-o-saurs

Some dinosaurs were carnivores.
Some dinosaurs were omnivores.
All dinosaurs are nevermores.
They are extinct,
No longer valid.
Perhaps they should have
Tried the salad.

Hand to Hand

The left hand asked the right hand,
"Why do *you* get all the fun?
You hold, you mold, you even fold.
You're treated number one.
You write, you draw, you open doors.
You weave and wave about.
You nab, you grab, you hail a cab.
And I just get *left* out."

Pass Out

I passed the soup. I passed the bread,
An ear of corn, a lettuce head.
I passed the punch. I passed the rice.
I passed the peas and carrots twice.
And when they passed to me at last,
I said, "No thanks, I think I'll pass."

Day Off

One dark and damp December morn
The sun refused to greet the dawn.
"I have no wish to see the sky—
All this pollution makes me cry.
The airplanes crowd around my head—
I'm going back to my warm bed,
Where I will sleep until it's June.
But meanwhile you can call the moon."

Bye Sky

I heard they sold
A piece of the sky.
They shipped it to
This creepy guy
Who said he'd put
The sky on cable
Or pay-per-view
If he is able.

Monster Menu

Soup
Staple soup seasoned to taste
With iron fillings and nuclear waste

Hors d'oeuvres
Candied ants in diesel dips
Served with fried computer chips

Entrée
Poached roach sautéed in slime
or
Legs of lizard stewed in grime

Dessert
Mouse mousse jubilee
Termite tea (caffeine-free)

Beware the Beast

Beware the beast
With seventeen feet
That silently shuffles
Its way down the street.
It never will roar
Or bellow or hiss.
It sneaks up behind you
While you're reading this.

Good Beds

Grandmother's couch
Kangaroo pouch
Soft mushy chair
Big friendly bear
A huge stack of hay
Your mom's macramé
A dozen koalas
A half-million dollars

Bad Beds

Bench in a park
Mouth of a shark
Garbage pails
Bed of nails
Elephant's trunk
In range of a skunk
Underneath birds
Near stampeding herds

Fish Story

Father and I went fishin' today.
We caught four fish, but one got away.
One got away—it's such a bother.
One got away and one got father!

Moon Boon

When the moon is just a sickle,
Then it eats a sour pickle.
When the moon shines like a crescent,
How it feasts upon a pheasant.
As it grows in size to half,
It consumes a whole giraffe.
While the moon becomes three-quarters,
Fifteen tons of fish it orders.
Later in its gibbous phase
Swallows whales with mayonnaise,
Till at last it's full and great,
Cleared the sky and cleaned its plate.
Everything in sight it ate.
Now it's time for losing weight.

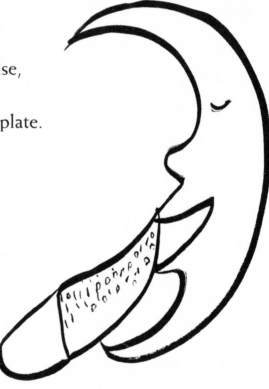

Plan-eat-ery

Here's the latest news from Mars:
  Mars is made of candy bars.
Here's the latest from the moon:
  The moon is one big macaroon.
Here's the latest news from Pluto:
  Pluto's core is pure prosciutto.
Here's the latest news from Earth:
  The earth's a peach, for what it's worth.

Funny Honey

You're my honey.
You're my sweet.
You're my pumpkin
Pie to eat.
You're my ice cream.
You're my ices.
You're my seasoning
And spices.
You're my candy.
You're my cake.
Oops! I ate you
By mistake!

Aunteater

My aunteater ate Aunt Antoinette,
Aunt Josephine, and Aunt Suzette,
Aunt Julianne just in from France,
And then my aunteater ran out of aunts.

Home Cookin'

Mother's meat loaf is so delicious
I feed my portion to the fishes.
Mother's roast is full of zest.
I always give mine to the guest.
Mother's pudding tastes so nice
I slip my bowl down to the mice.
Mother's spaghetti has me agog.
I fork mine over to the dog.
Mother's cooking is beyond compare.
Her dishes are riches you simply *must* share.

So On and So Forth

Life is precious.
Life is short.
Life's a lily.
Life's a wart.
Life is cool.
Life is crazy.
April fool.
Whoops
    a
        daisy.

Pig Out

Said Papa Pig to his daughter Pauline,
"Go mess up your room. It's much too clean!"

Good Conduct

Matthew made his teacher mad.
Teacher called his conduct bad.
Bratty Matty was aloof—
Climbed from classroom to the roof,
Where he threw his socks and shoes
Onto people to amuse,
Till a passing lightning bolt
Shot through Matthew with a jolt,
Which at least proved Teacher wrong:
Matthew's conduct WAS quite strong.

Partly

Partly cloudy,
Partly sun.
Today the weather
Is partly done.

Weather Wise

The weather went on strike today.
The sky will not be blue or gray.
Nor will the clouds or sun be seen.
Next report at 10:15.

Noah Noted

It's rained for forty days without miss.
It doesn't get any wetter than this.

Open Mind

It's good to have an open mind,
So I pried mine open
And what did I find?
A dirty mop,
A map of Guam,
Report cards that I hid from Mom,
A checker piece,
A chicken bone,
A tube of toothpaste
Hard as stone,
A tennis ball,
A tennis court,
Last year's missing
Book report,
A lucky pin,
A leaking pen,
A song we knew
From way back when,
A cockatoo,
A coconut—
Sometimes a mind
Is best left shut.

Brain Drain

If your brain is all befuddled,
Dazed and crazed and all bemuddled,
If you find it hard to think,
Throw your brain inside the sink.
Rub and scrub it in hot water
With your brother and your daughter.
With your uncles and your nieces,
Iron out those little creases.
When it's smooth as gingerbread
Stick it back inside your head.

This poem entitles thee
to one million dollars
completely tax-free
in fresh crispy bills
straight from the mint,
but only play money—
Always read the
fine print.

Brat Chat

Little Lauren was such a brat
That she was turned into a cat.
And now the sorry little bosser
Drinks her milk out of a saucer.
And now the tired little bore
Has to sleep inside a drawer.
And now the girl who was not nice
Eats for dinner little mice.

George ignored his mother's wish—
He was turned into a fish.
Didn't bathe inside the tub,
Now he's underwater—*glub*.
He refused to cut his nails—
Now he's sporting fins and scales.
Always playing pranks and larks,
Now he's dodging rays and sharks.

Children, heed your folks and teacher,
Pastor, rabbi, priest, or preacher,
Or YOU'LL turn into a creature.

I-Turn, U-Turn

I made a left turn
And then a right;
I made a you-turn:
I'm you tonight!

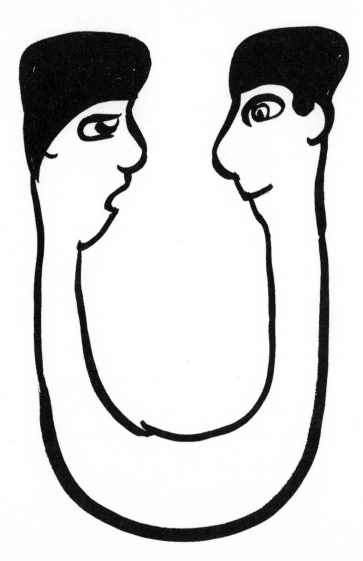

Bad Hair Day

I'm having a very bad hair day today
'Cause some of my hairs began to turn gray
And purple and pink and chartreuse and red.
I think I'll go buy a big hat for my head.

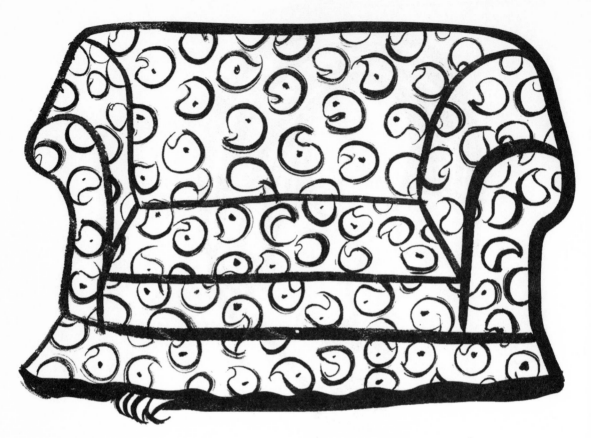

Unsafe Sofa

Under the sofa
There's something alive.
Its green teeth are gruesome
And sharper than knives.
Its skin is infected,
All covered with blisters.
It swallowed my homework
And both of my sisters.
It has purple pimples
And steel wool for hair.
So if you don't mind,
I will sit on the CHAIR.

Homebody

The bluebird's home is in a nest.
The lion's in its lair.
The ants are found
Inside their mound.
My dad lives in his chair.

Couch Potatoes

Couch potatoes don't need hands.
Don't need legs; they never stand.
Don't need elbows, knees, or thighs.
Couch potatoes just need eyes.

Cruel Rule

Once great dinosaurs did rule.
Now they're only fossil fuel.

Dinostory

An ordinary dinosaur
Is high as seven floors or more
And bangs its head against the door,
Which makes it very dino-sore.

Dinohurry

When dinosaurs are in a hurry,
They step on creatures as they scurry—
Which makes them very dino-sorry.

The Dreaded Dreeth

The dreaded Dreeth
Has eighty-odd teeth:
Twenty above
And twenty beneath,
Twenty more left
And twenty more right—
A toothsome,
Gruesome,
Chewsome sight.

What I'd Like to Share

I'd like to share a nasty cold
And all my clothing that's too old.
I'd like to share my toys that broke,
At dinnertime, my artichoke.
I'd like to share a rotten chore.
Perhaps you'd like to sweep the floor?
And I would gladly share the pain
Of toothaches or an ankle sprain.
I'd share my cares,
My worries, too.
I thought I'd share
These thoughts with you.

Digital Dude

I'm a digital dude
In a digital mood.
I eat digital food.
It gets digital chewed
On a digital plate.
It tastes digital great.
I eat digital meat
With a digital beet
In my digital seat.
Then I digital walk
Or I digital talk
On my digital phone
In my digital home
With my digital wife.
It's a digital life.

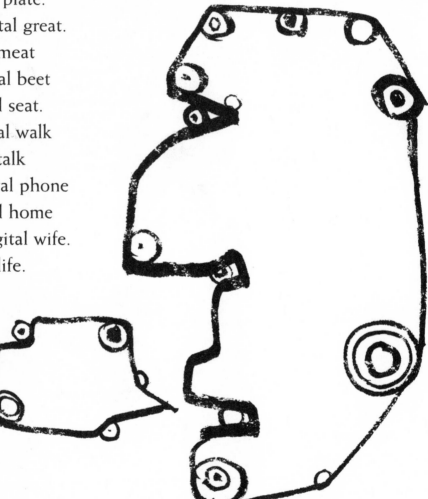

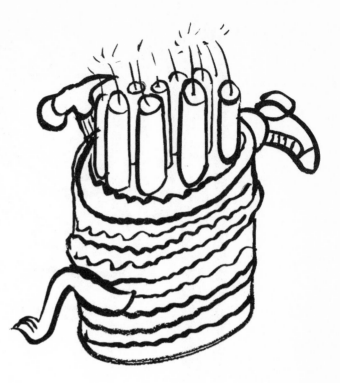

Burpday Cake

My sister made a birthday cake.
She put in pennies by mistake.
Instead of half a cup of flour
She threw in half a dozen flowers.
Instead of seven spoons of yeast,
A toenail from a wildebeest.
Instead of salt,
Her pet frog, Walt.
For added spice,
Some purple lice
And her doll's shoe
And airplane glue.
I don't want any.
How 'bout you?

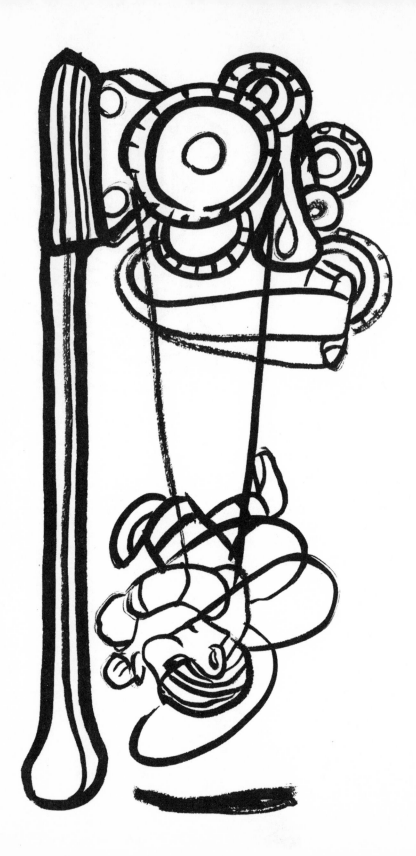

Inventions I'd Like to See

A bully-pulley
  A diaper-wiper
    A teacher-screecher
      A cold-feet-heater
        A homework-shirker
          An annoyer-destroyer
            A sister-twister
              A whiner-entwiner
                A pester-ingester
                  A bragger-dragger
                    A blabber-grabber
                      A weekend-extender
                        A go-to-bed-shredder

School Schedule

At nine o'clock we studied history,
But what we learned is still a mystery.
By ten the class moved on to math,
And waited for the aftermath.
That was followed by biology.
We fell asleep without apology.
English was the next we'd study—
Our brains turned into Silly Putty,
Till, at last, the lunch bell rang. . . .
We woke!
We spoke!
We ran!
We sang!

Pizza Treatsa

I love to eatsa
Chewy pizza,
Standing up
Or in a seatsa.
A neatsa pizza
Can't be beatsa.
Eat it with your
Hands or feetsa.

Pass the Pizza

I made a pizza
But had no spice—
I thought it might taste just as nice.
I made a pizza
But had no cheese.
Instead I threw in frozen peas.
I made a pizza
But had no tomatoes.
Instead I tried home fried potatoes.
I made a pizza
Without any dough.
Why people like pizza
I really don't know.

Reptile Style

A python looks nice on
Your head as a hat.
A great conversation piece
Upon which to chat.
Its colors are pretty.
Its contours are nice.
It's easy to feed it
With two or three mice.
It's warm in the winter,
Protects from the rain.
At parties and functions
It can entertain.
It frightens rude people
And any stray bat.
A python looks nice on
Your head as a hat.

The Eels

Eels are smart.
They aren't fools.
They go to eelementary schools.

Stupid Stew

I'm stirring up my stupid stew.
My head gets dumber the more I chew.
I'm dim and dull but when I'm through
I'm still not half as dumb as you!

Semi-poem

This poem is done
Before it starts.
My sister stole
The other parts.

Food Mood

I shake and I shiver,
Just thinking of liver.
I cowardly cower
When near cauliflower.
I break out in hives
Within range of chives.
I quickly retreat
If you serve me a beet.
I soon will get lost
To avoid applesauce.
I whine and I wheeze
When thinking of cheese,
And don't give me peas—
Please!
Please!

School Lunch

Our school lunch is from outer space,
Endangering the human race.
The meatballs bounce right off the floor.
The fish cakes could break down a door.
The bread was baked ten years ago.
The burgers look like they will grow.
The chicken has the chicken pox.
The peas are frozen in the box.
The spinach gives your legs gangrene.
The fruit juice tastes like gasoline.
The soup is salty as the sea.
The franks explode like TNT.
The salad bar—don't dare to try it.
The carrot cake once caused a riot.
The deadly tuna casserole
Can bore a hole right through the bowl.
The fries could knock you off your chair.
The corn could make you lose your hair.
The way they cook here is a crime,

But lunch is still my favorite time.

C.B. & J.B.

C.B. & J.B.
Met B.B. & A.B.,
And K.B. & B.C.
Met D.C. & D.D.
These A.B.'s
& B.C.'s
& C.D.'s
& J.B.'s
Are giving to
Me Me
The worst
Heebie-jeebies.

Substitute Teacher

Today we had a substitute.
She wasn't sweet.
She wasn't cute.
Her hair could scare a ghastly ghost.
Her breath could turn bread into toast.
She barely fit inside the door
And looked much like a dinosaur.
Each time she spoke the windows shook,
And when she read she broke the book.
She didn't have a lesson plan
But walked like an orangutan.
And if someone would misbehave,
Her screams could start a tidal wave.
But if you think that SHE'S a creature,
Wait till you meet our REGULAR teacher.

Witches' Wishes

Witches wish for
Rusty nails,
Dusty cupboards,
Dragon tails.
Nasty weather,
Storm and flood,
Vulture feather,
Vampire blood.
Squeaky hinges,
Broken glass,
Beetle binges,
Burned-out grass.
Poison ivy,
Pumpkin seeds,
Skin all hivey,
Ugly weeds.
Spiderwebs on
Dirty dishes.
Witches always
Get their wishes.

Once a Year

Once a year is Halloween,
When ghosts and goblins
And witches are seen.
They screech and scream
Across the nation.
The rest of the year
They're on vacation.

Tragic Magic

Magicians never die—
It's true.
They simply disappear from view.

If You Suffer Smelly Feet

If you suffer smelly feet,
Let them air out in the street.
Throw them in the washing machine—
That will leave them fresh and clean.
Hang them on the laundry line,
Then your feet will smell just fine.

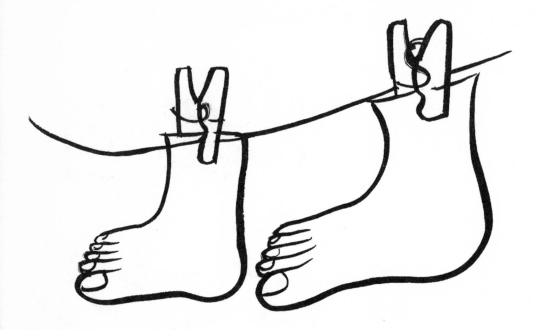

Rose Nose

A rose by any other name,
They say, would smell as sweet.
But still, I think,
That it would stink,
If we called roses feet.

A Lot Dog

Give me a hot dog
With *everything* on it:
A french fry,
A necktie,
A baseball,
A bonnet.
A jaguar,
A crowbar,
A gallon of custard.
An ice tray,
A highway,
But please hold the mustard.

Monster Meatballs

Monster meatballs
So scary to chew.
First you bite THEM,
Then they bite YOU.

Group Coupon

Send in your coupons: fifty cents off,
And we'll speed you a brand new cough.
And if you order now two sneezes,
We'll gladly throw in four diseases.

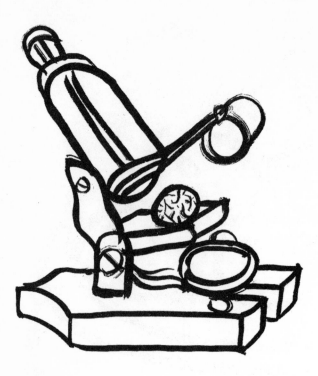

Lead Head

Your head is full of lead.
Your head is made of soap.
To see your pea-size brain I'd need
To use a microscope.

Don't Drink Ink

Don't drink ink
(Green or tangerine or pink).
Ink will make your insides stink.
Don't drink ink!

Some Nieces Are Nice

Some nieces are nasty.
Some nieces are nice.
My niece named Clarisse
Should go skate on thin ice.

True Love

I love you each and every way.
I love you more each passing day.
That, plus the other kids ran away.

Directions to the End of the World

Turn left.
Turn right.
Turn the day into the night.
Hit the gas.
Hit the brake.
Hit your sister by mistake.
Change the oil.
Change a tire.
Change your name to Myron Meyer.
Stop for water.
Stop for food.
Stop to bite your nails — it's rude.
Drive fast.
Drive slow.
Drive into a bungalow.
When you see straight
At the bend
Then you'll know you're at
THE END.

The Tide

The tide comes in.
The tide goes out.
And by the beach
The tide hangs out.
It *tidies* up
The shore by hand,
Then *waves* good-bye
To shell and sand.

Worse Verse

I read some verse.
It was the worst.
I threw it in the ocean.
It sank like lead
To the seabed—
Like poetry in motion.

Silly Pilly

If you feel sick,
If you feel ill,
Try swallowing
This ten-pound pill.
It's fortified with lizard knee,
The eye of newt,
Extract of bee.
It satisfies your daily need
For rhubarb root
And maple seed.
With wild weeds and five raw eggs,
It helps you grow
Grass on your legs.
It clears your head,
It clears your skin,
And if you're fat,
It makes you thin.
So open wide and bottoms up!
Just gulp it down—
And don't throw up.

Don't Drag a Dragon

Don't drag a dragon by its tail,
Or you might break its fingernail.
And if its fingernail you crack,
It just might eat you for a snack.
Don't drag a dragon by its tooth.
To drag it such is most uncouth,
Discourteous, and impolite,
And it will eat you in one bite.
Don't drag a dragon by its claws.
Why?
Because.

Hero-ex

A dragon was hungry
To eat something rich,
So it swallowed a hero
In a hero sandwich.

Grow Up!

The grown-ups told him, "Grow up!"
But he started growing down.
His legs grew shoots.
His feet grew roots
That sank into the ground.
His arms branched out.
His hands did sprout.
Great leaves rose from his head.
The grown-ups told him, "Grow up!"
They got a tree instead.

Package Deal

Pachyderm's nose: elephant trunk
Packed with clothes: traveler's trunk
Packed by snows: tree trunk

Ghost Host

A vastly
    ghastly
        nasty ghost
Flew in Friday
From the coast.
It scared every Mrs.
            Ms.
            and
        Mr.
But let out a shriek
When it saw my sister.

Why?

Why did the ghastly ghost say *boo*?
    It got a closer look at you.
Why did the monster screech and scream?
    It saw your face inside a dream.
Why did the witch fly on her broom?
    She took a peek inside your room.
What gave all the ghouls a scare?
    They saw you in your underwear.

Karate Kids

One was a black belt.
One was a brown.
One had a loose belt;
His pants fell down.

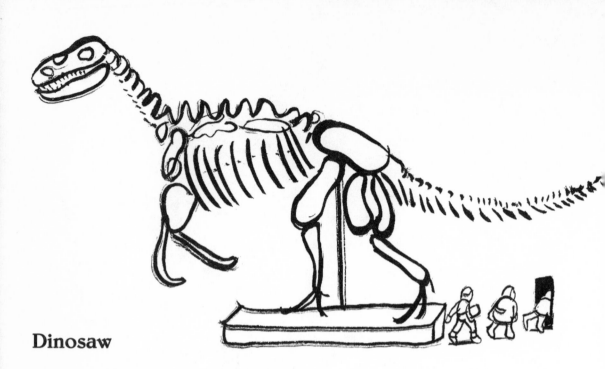

Dinosaw

Dinosaur bones sit in the museum.
Children come each day to see 'em.
Dinosaur bones live on and on,
Long after all the children have gone.

Camels

Camels have one hump.
Camels have two.
Camels have three humps. . . .
(Do I have the flu?)

Today's Weather

Rain, hail,
Garbage pails.
Snow, sleet,
Chicken feet.
Drizzle, mist,
Optometrists.
Cloudy, showers,
Cauliflowers.
Later clearing
With an earring.

DON'T!

Don't slurp
Your soup.
Don't burp.
Don't stoop.
Don't fidget.
Don't fumble.
Don't mutter.
Don't mumble.
Don't dream.
Don't doze.
Don't pick
Your nose.
Don't whine.
Don't wheeze.
Don't snivel.
Don't sneeze.
Don't bite.
Don't brawl.
DON'T NOTHING AT ALL!

Do-It-Yourself Poem

I didn't have time to finish this poem,
So **you** can write it in your _____.
Fill in a word, a rhyme or two.
It isn't very hard to _____.
Keep the rhythm and the beat.
Keep each sentence short and _____.
Now, at last, this poem must end.
Thank you very much, my _____.

Cute Suit

See my sixty-three-piece suit,
So swank it slinks
And stinks to boot.
I am François,
The fresh-fishmonger.
At least I'll never
Die from hunger.

Monstory

A monster with a mirror
Was so grouchy
      grim and
        gruff,
It said, "I'm going back to bed,
I don't look ugly enough!"

Monster Meal

I invited a monster for a meal
Of chicken fat and orange peel.
It nibbled into cherry pits
And gobbled boiled beetle bits.
It savored seven slimy slugs
Flavored with five ladybugs.
It crunched a crate
And munched a moth,
Then ate its plate
And tablecloth.
It swallowed the table as well as the chair,
Along with all the silverware,
Then all the walls,
The floor and door—
I won't invite that beast no more.

Mr. Medd and Mr. Redd

Mr. Medd and Mr. Redd
Thought they would put together heads.
But rotten luck—
Their heads got stuck.
Some days don't pay
To get out of bed.

Caveat to a Brat

If at first you don't succeed,
Cry, cry again.

Shoes

First you
    Choose shoes.
        Then you
            Use shoes.
                Next you
                    Bruise shoes
                        And abuse shoes
                      Till you
                        Lose shoes.
                          Say *adieus* to
                            Your once-new shoes.

Dinomore

The dinosaur was a giant beast:
Its head was west, its tail was east.
How fortunate it's now deceased.

T. Rex

It doesn't take cash.
It doesn't take checks.
It only takes arms
And legs
And necks.

Steak Mistake

How do you like your steak, sir?
Broiled? Boiled? Still covered with fur?

Quick Picnic

Forgot the bread.
Forgot the juice.
Forgot the napkins
And Uncle Bruce.
Forgot the book.
Forgot the game.
But all the ants came
Just the same.

Who Knew Newton?

An apple fell
On Sir Isaac Newton.
Did it hurt?
Did it smart?
You're darn tootin'.
More than a blister.
More than a cavity:
A small price to pay
For discovering gravity.

Hello, My Name Is Dracula

Hello, my name is Dracula.
My clothing is all blackula.
I drive a Cadillacula.
I am a maniacula.
I drink blood for a snackula.
Your neck I will attackula
With teeth sharp as a tackula.
At dawn I hit the sackula.
Tomorrow I'll be backula!

Out from Darkest Transylvania

Out from darkest Transylvania
Comes a man, a man with a mania:
He's looking for blood—
Type A, B, or O.
He'll drink sitting down
Or take it to go.
He's not very tall.
His skin is quite pale,
But going for blood,
He'll fight tooth and nail!

UFO

Are UFOs our friend or foe?
Inquiring minds all want to know.
Did aliens race a zillion miles
Just to see us earthlings smile?
Or do they have an evil plan:
To put us in a roasting pan
And take us back to their home planet
To serve us with a pomegranate?

Sigh-clops

I saw an ugly cyclops.
I punched him in the eyeclops.
Then he began to cryclops.
So I said, "Hush-a-byeclops!"
And sang a lullabyeclops,
Shook hands and said, "Good-byeclops."

Good Wood

I ate an elm for lunch today,
An oak just for a joke.
I slept for hours
On beds of flowers,
Burped swallows when I woke.

Treetice

A tree has bark
But cannot bark.
It cannot move.
It has to park.

A tree has roots
But cannot root.
A tree has shoots
But cannot shoot.

A tree has limbs
But is not limber.
Some are lumber.
Some are timber.
TIMMMMBERRRR!

Pebbles, Peoples

A pebble used to be a rock.
A rock was once a boulder.
I guess that pebbles are like us . . .
They shrink as they get older.

There Was an Old Woman Named Rose

There was an old woman named Rose,
Who had a humongous nose.
   On a wide avenue
   It blocked off half her view,
And she had trouble seeing her toes.

There Was a Young Person Named Blair

There was a young person named Blair,
Who grew several plants in his hair.
    He raised red tomatoes,
     Green peas, and potatoes,
And kept a small gardener up there.

Limo Seen

Have you seen my limousine?
It's larger than an ark.
It seats one hundred seventeen.
It's very hard to park.

Keep Your Eyes

Keep your eyes
Off my fries.
Keep your knees
Off my peas.
Keep your belly
Off my jelly.
Keep your hair
Off my pear.
Keep your legs
Off my eggs.
And *please*, keep your brain
Off my chow mein.

Rules of Speaking

When speaking, you should always stand,
But not on someone else's hand.
Don't bite your nails or suck your thumb.
Refrain from saying, "Um, um, um."
Speak in a voice both clear and deep,
And cover those who fall asleep.

Question to a Basketball Player

What do you have
Inside those shoes?
Springs?
Wings?
Kangaroos?

Shuttle Scuttle

Because of a decimal point
In the wrong place,
They fired Florida
Off into space.

Class Clown

Barney Brown is our class clown—
He always makes the teacher frown.
One day he brought a snake to school.
The other kids thought that was cool.
Upon his desk he wrote a word
That decent children haven't heard.
He chews ten wads of bubble gum.
While Teacher talks, he loves to hum.
At lunch he spits out all his peas
Across the room with greatest ease.
He scrapes his nails across the board.
The first three months of school he snored.
He sees the principal so much,
He pays him room and board and such.
He's not a fool. He's our class clown—
Until the circus comes to town.

Food for Thought

A lettuce head
Can never think.
Potato eyes
Can never blink.
An ear of corn
Can never hear.
My appetite
Is gone, I fear.

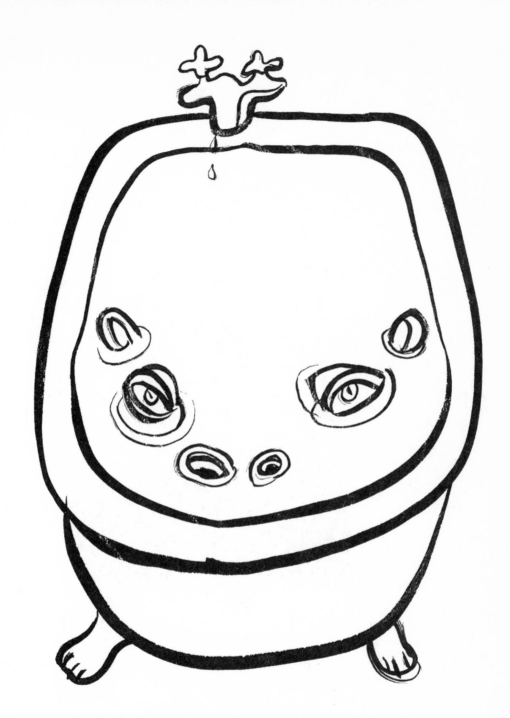

Anonymous

It's hard to be anonymous
When you're a hippopotamus.

Alien Lullaby

The stars are out.
It's time for bed.
Lay down your head,
And head,
And head.

Index of Titles

Index of First Lines

Other Books by Douglas Florian